HAPPY AS MICHAEL TEACHINGS

Learning to Embrace What Is

SHEPHERD HOODWIN

Summerjoy Press
LAGUNA NIGUEL, CALIFORNIA

HAPPINESS AND THE MICHAEL TEACHINGS
Learning to Embrace What is

Summerjoy Press
99 Pearl
Laguna Niguel CA 92677-4818

shoodwin@gmail.com
https://shepherdhoodwin.com

Copyright © 2015, 2020 by Shepherd Hoodwin

All rights reserved. No part of this publication may be reproduced, stored in a retrieval system, or transmitted, in any form or by any means, electronic, mechanical, photocopying, recording, or otherwise, without the prior written permission of the publisher, except by a reviewer, who may quote brief passages in a review.

ISBN: 9798651853281

Photograph of Shepherd Hoodwin by John Kilis.

Dedicated to

Patricia Kendall

*My Brilliant Friend Who Introduced Me
To the Michael Teachings*

INTRODUCTION

The Michael teachings are an extraordinary body of channeled material that paint a vivid portrait of how we, as eternal souls, set up our lifetimes—why we're here, what our lessons are, and how we can learn them more efficiently and joyfully.

I am a Michael channel. My site (Shepherd-Hoodwin.com) links to several Michael books I've written. This short one explores how we can use the teachings to increase our happiness, which ultimately is the aim of every spiritual path.

Happiness is too important to leave to chance or circumstance. I sometimes joke that I'm determined to learn to be happy even if it kills me! They say that we teach what we most want to learn. I have been giving a good deal of thought about what it takes to be happy, and by working on this book, I have been clarifying happiness for myself; I hope it aids you, too.

In Part I, we'll explore the mechanics of happiness. In Part II, we'll look at some happiness skills. In Part III, we'll go through the roles and overleaves, which are part of the Michael teachings, and discuss happiness as it pertains to each of them.

Many thanks to Lauren Jensen for transcribing the lecture upon which this piece is based.

> Shepherd Hoodwin
> Laguna Niguel, California
> June 20, 2020

CONTENTS

INTRODUCTION — iv

I THE MECHANICS OF HAPPINESS — 1

- 1 • THREE LEVELS OF HAPPINESS — 3
- 2 • FREEDOM AND REFINEMENT — 4
- 3 • GRATITUDE — 5
- 4 • POLARITY — 6
- 5 • ESSENCE — 9
- 6 • JUDGMENTALNESS — 10
- 7 • KARMA — 12
- 8 • ACCURATE EXPECTATIONS — 14
- 9 • EVIL — 16
- 10 • CHOICE — 18

II HAPPINESS SKILLS — 20

- 11 • FRAMING OUR EXPERIENCES — 21
- 12 • TAKING ACTION — 22
- 13 • OUR GIFTS — 24
- 14 • RESPECTING EMOTIONS — 26
- 15 • LIFE SKILLS — 27
- 16 • UNDERSTANDING OUR DIFFERENCES — 28
- 17 • POSITIVE POLES — 29
- 18 • BALANCING TRUE REST, PLAY, STUDY, AND WORK — 31

CONTENTS

19 • LIFE TASK 32
20 • NINE NEEDS 33
21 • EVOLUTION 34
22 • MODELING LOVE 36
III USING YOUR OVERLEAVES 37
23 • ROLES 38
24 • GOALS 41
25 • ATTITUDES 43
26 • MODES 46
27 CENTERS 48
28 • OBSTACLES 50
29 • BODY TYPES 53
CONCLUSION 55
BACK MATTER 56
ABOUT THE AUTHOR 57
OTHER BOOKS BY SHEPHERD HOODWIN 59
REVIEWS 64

Part I

THE MECHANICS OF HAPPINESS

Some people seem to come by happiness easily. Either they have a naturally sunny disposition, and/or their life has had relatively few bumps in the road. However, happiness is partly a skill, and we can all improve our happiness chops with practice, as well as by cultivating perspectives that foster it. It is a particularly interesting challenge to start out as someone to whom happiness doesn't come easily and learn to be happy.

1 • THREE LEVELS OF HAPPINESS

The spiritual aspect of happiness might be referred to as joy. Joy is the surest indicator of spiritual advancement—not how much knowledge we have, our psychic abilities, or our soul age. Joy is the highest manifestation of our positive poles, the clearest indication of essence contact.

Joy could be defined as the free and refined expression of self through our spirit: our energy isn't blocked but neither is it out of control. A core Michael teaching is that all experience, whether joyful or painful, can lead to growth. By becoming more conscious, however, we can choose to grow more through joy and less through pain.

The free and refined expression of self through the personality (mind and emotions) is usually what is meant by happiness. Through the body, we might call it pleasure. Joy, happiness, and pleasure are each beautiful and important to our evolution.

The words used don't matter; there can also be mental and emotional pleasure, for instance. In this book, I'm going to use the word "happiness" more generally to refer to the free and refined expression of self through all three levels, since the mechanics are similar with each. Body, personality, and spirit aren't separate—they are the three aspects of self.

2 • FREEDOM AND REFINEMENT

Just as our muscles must both contract and expand, flex and relax, in balance, for us to move, happiness requires both refinement and freedom. Freedom is the cardinal, or expanded, side of happiness. It allows a larger *quantity* of self to come through because there aren't barriers. Refinement is the ordinal, or contracted, side: it allows a higher *quality* of self to come through because there is mastery over its expression. If we open up to too much quantity without quality, we can get to a point where there's no control and happiness dissipates, like a child who laughs hysterically and ends up crying. If there's too much quality (control) without quantity (freedom), happiness can be blocked because we're tense.

3 • GRATITUDE

Spiritual teachings often emphasize gratitude. Gratitude increases happiness because when we are grateful for something, we embrace it—we love and approve of it—so our energy flows freely through us out to it. It especially affects the quantity side of happiness, but gratitude has a high vibration, so it also improves quality.

Gratitude can exist on all three levels. When our body likes something, such as being touched affectionately, it is grateful for it. Our life force flows out to it, and it forms a circuit with the life force flowing from the other person. That movement of energy gives us pleasure.

When we embrace something intellectually and emotionally, recognizing and appreciating its value, our personality energy flows out to it, forming a circuit that gives us happiness. Emotions are the substance of our personality, and thoughts are the containers. Emotional healing is a large part of creating happiness, because when our emotions are stuck, this flow cannot occur.

4 • POLARITY

The body and personality live on the physical plane, which is a plane of polarity (opposites): light/dark, female/male, sweet/sour, etc. In polarity, we are always weighing things, trying to discern one thing versus another so that we can learn. The goal isn't to get rid of polarity, which isn't possible; the goal is to use it constructively. Polarity itself has polarities—it can be used in either a positive (constructive) or negative (destructive) way.

The body naturally moves toward pleasure and away from pain. In the negative pole, it goes out of balance and becomes addicted—it loses refinement in favor of freedom, which becomes license; it gains quantity but loses quality. Or it gains quality but loses quantity by becoming anxious because it is afraid of pain.

The mind uses polarity as comparisons; mental gratitude might compare how much better off we are than others. This can be useful for putting our life into perspective. However, being grateful only because others seem to have it worse can lead to comparisons with those who seem to have it better and complaining about it, which isn't useful to building happiness. It judges one's present situation as being wanting rather than loving it as it is. It gains quality (discernment) at the expense of quantity—love stops flowing. Or the mind goes out of balance in the cardinal direction by gaining quantity, being overenthusiastic about the thing it judges good, and losing quality (discernment).

Emotional polarities are similarly built on

comparisons. Let's say that one's partner is enjoying someone else's friendship. Emotional gratitude might frame this as one's circle of love expanding, making more love for all three of them. If one is insecure and contracts, one may become jealous: the comparison concludes that one is getting the short end of the stick. The opposite imbalance could lead to a lack of healthy boundaries. The way we frame our experiences is as important to our happiness as the experiences themselves.

Essence is our core, our potential that resonates with the three high (abstract) planes where love, truth, and beauty are directly experienced. It sees all experiences as part of our journey of evolution through the universe. The highest form of gratitude is the gratitude of essence. Essence loves and is grateful for everything—it is outside polarity. When we experience that, seeing the perfection in all things, it brings joy.

Our soul is the outer layer of essence that incarnates. It straddles the physical and astral planes. There is much less polarity on the astral. Therefore, our spirit, the emanation of our soul, is capable of pure, unconditional gratitude, without comparisons.

Nature demonstrates unconditional gratitude. Trees, for example, don't have any judgments against their environment. There are no barriers, so we enjoy that rich oxygen, which is an expression of pure gratitude by the trees, while they enjoy the carbon dioxide we exhale. Our experience of pure gratitude is similar.

In unconditional gratitude we see the value of everything, even if it is something we don't like. All experiences can teach and deepen us. We look at all people and see that they are perfect exactly the way they are. They provide lessons for themselves and others, and are growing toward their potential.

It doesn't serve our happiness to pretend that we like something we don't. It does serve it to embrace what is, changing what we can and making the best of what we cannot. We need not contract our energy because we don't like something. Finding some way to keep it flowing even in uncomfortable situations is a key to happiness.

5 • ESSENCE

As our consciousness rises into alignment with essence, we are better able to transcend polarity and therefore use it constructively. We are no longer controlled by it, tossed from one extreme to another. We no longer participate in the illusory war of good versus evil. We reside in equanimity. We discern the polarities, but see everything as a perfect part of the whole. Being human, we still have likes and dislikes, but they aren't extreme or inflexible.

Michael teaches that growth occurs through essence contact. Essence is ultimately what we are. Our experiences are the raw material for growth, but the actual growth occurs when we open it up to the light of essence. That is how we transform our soul from a lump of coal into a diamond. That is what joy is.

6 • JUDGMENTALNESS

Judgmentalness is the negative side of polarity (discernment is the positive). The Garden of Eden story (and similar stories in cultures all over the world) says that humans were kicked out when they ate of the fruit of the tree of knowledge of good and evil. A lot of people interpret that as meaning that when humans gained knowledge (intellect), they lost the garden. But that's not what it says—it says the knowledge of *good and evil*; in other words, when humans became judgmental (and started withholding love).

Discernment, seeing "this" versus "that," isn't itself judgmental. Jesus suggested that we be wise as serpents (and gentle as doves). A serpent resembles a brain and spinal cord. We're supposed to think—just not judgmentally. Discernment is a vital part of the growth of consciousness.

Judgmentalness, however, lacks compassion and understanding. It points the finger. It arbitrarily classifies some things as being good to the exclusion of others, fragmenting the whole and confining parts of reality. It makes some things wrong simply for being what they are. Everyone has different ideas about what is good and evil. Some churches believe that dancing on Sundays is evil, for instance. Disliking something is a personal truth; judging it as evil tries to turn it into a universal truth, when it may not be. Dancing on Sundays is in the eye of the beholder; committing karma is not.

Judgmentalness pervades humanity, and has for a very long time. It's difficult to step out of that mindset where we are constantly judging ourselves and others. If we are judging ourselves, we are surely judging others as well, even if we aren't conscious of it. And if we are judging others, we are surely judging ourselves, even if we aren't conscious of it.

Why are we so judgmental? It relates to our animal-level hardwiring, automatic mechanisms designed to keep us safe. A stranger or someone who seems different might pose a threat, so our unthinking reaction is suspicion and criticism—we look for danger. These simplistic mechanisms are designed to be foolproof, to operate when "nobody's home." They are embedded into our brain and spinal cord—the serpent. The serpent has been blamed for the fall of man because it influenced Eve (emotions) who, in turn, influenced Adam (intellect). However, the personality need not be controlled by hardwiring. When somebody is home, we can make more sophisticated evaluations and choices. Then we can dismantle our automatic, predictable reactions. As we become more conscious, we become less judgmental. The tendencies of the human animal are gradually supplanted by those of the incarnate soul. With discernment, we're awake and see what is, apart from biological and societal biases.

7 • KARMA

Karma is a natural law that stands outside subjective judgments. Negative karma is violating others, such as killing or robbing. If you commit karma, you experience the consequences. Something isn't karmic because of a person's subjective judgment that it's evil; it's karmic because there is a factual violation that shows up in the energy. However, even negative karma is included in the perfection of what is—it's part of how we grow. When we insist that something shouldn't be the way it is when it *is* the way it is, we set up a contraction in ourselves. It's more useful to fully feel our pain without resistance so that our energy can move.

There are some karmic acts so shockingly heinous that it's hard to believe that someone would commit them. We may be temporarily stunned into inaction because they are far outside our usual reality, and then the actions we take may be inappropriate or, at least, unhelpful. However, the quicker we grok that they did, in fact, happen, that they're part of reality, the quicker we can discern them and take appropriate actions.

In a sense, this is a loss of innocence, but the existence of extreme karma doesn't negate the existence of love, truth, and beauty. We need not become soured on life because we encountered something heinous. Ultimately, even that serves our evolution because it brings into sharper focus what love, truth, and beauty are.

Accepting what is, even when it is horrible, frees

us to move on. Revising our view of reality can be stressful, but being frozen in resistance makes us victims, stuck in the past. In fact, anytime someone disappoints us because we had expected different behavior, the quicker we revise our expectations to match the facts, the happier we can be. When we're disillusioned, it's helpful to frame that as gaining useful new information that will help us work more effectively with what is. We had expected one thing—naively, it turns out—but now we have a better idea of what we're really dealing with.

8 • ACCURATE EXPECTATIONS

We live in a highly imperfect world, and each of us has many flaws. The paradox is that all these imperfections are perfect just the way they are as starting points for what is to come. We can only start from where we are. And if were already perfect, we'd have nothing to do.

True acceptance is not being complacent or passive, but simply being peaceful and embracing the opportunities for creativity that our challenges give us. Maybe they are not the opportunities we would prefer—they often aren't—but we just waste energy lamenting that. When we react negatively to annoyances, it's a good idea to ask ourselves, "Is this worth giving up my happiness?"

Embracing "what is" is actually the fastest way to create the future we'd prefer to live in. This isn't really positive thinking—it is practical thinking. Sometimes negative thinking is also useful, if it gives us an accurate picture of what is. Sometimes positive thinking is a hindrance, if it leads to denial of what is. Both positive and negative thinking are useful if they lead to acceptance and constructive action. The measure of our thinking isn't whether it is positive, but whether it's useful, although positive thinking is usually more useful and accurate than negative—there's usually *something* we can do. Sometimes strategic withdrawal is called for to give us a chance to regroup, but giving in to defeat is almost never in our best interests.

Humanity is a long way from enlightenment. We're better off being realistic about the generally low consciousness of people. Rather than wasting energy with excessive, chronic shock and outrage (such as about politics), it's more useful to concentrate on being a source of constructive change. The news is full of the same-old-same-old—there's not much new about it. This week's car chase isn't much different from last week's. This month's fill-in-the-blanks "scandal" isn't materially different from last month's. Why are we shocked? It is as though we expected humanity to be elevated, and keep being surprised and angry that it isn't. We've already had plenty of evidence that it's not. Many people are addicted to adenalin—they like being angry; it makes them feel alive, in contrast to their normally dulled senses. But being agitated isn't being happy.

If we view life as the school for souls that it is (among other things), we can take full advantage of the education it affords. If we think that life exists only to give us what we want and make us comfortable, we will be continually disappointed. There's nothing wrong with getting what we want and being comfortable, but we can't count on that happening. We can only count on our ability to embrace whatever comes and make the best of it.

9 • EVIL

Seeking to compassionately understand human shortcomings in general helps us understand ourselves. We're all in this together. "Good versus evil," a meme that pervades popular culture, presumes that evil is only outside us. Evil is simply the part of all of us that is not yet evolved, that is still in darkness. (See my book, *Compassion for Evil*, at my site.) Embracing our own unevolved shadows allows us to be a true force for good.

When someone does something egregious, he is at a particular level of consciousness and may not know any better at that point. If we really know better, not just intellectually but in our being, we generally do better.

Intellectually, we might say, "I shouldn't eat that piece of cake because I'm on a diet," but then eat it anyway. We haven't yet gotten to the point where our whole being really understands and is in equilibrium, where we can easily make the choices that are best for our health. So, in a sense, we don't know better, at least not entirely. When we've come to a deep balance and clarity around food, it's relatively easy to make wise choices without a lot of willpower. Good is not battling evil in us; the emotional charge is gone. It's not cut-and-dried, though, because our bodies are hardwired to seek sweets, dating from a time when they were hard to find, so some self-control may still be needed. There can also be metabolic factors, such as our body seeking a quick boost of energy. We need not judge ourselves when we "fail." The most useful approach is to learn from

9 • EVIL

it, plan better future strategies, and move on.

That's a trivial example, but those who do heinous things usually don't truly know better, either. This doesn't excuse their actions—we're all responsible for our choices and must accept the consequences. However, it's more useful to understand how they may have been damaged and might be helped, rather than taking a merely adversarial approach to them. On the level of the two-dimensional war of good versus evil, there is no solution, because most people think they're the good guys, or at least rationalize their behavior. Healing must come from a higher place of compassion that addresses causes.

Once someone is classified as being evil, withholding love seems justified. After all, evil people don't deserve love, do they? However, withholding love harms the withholder as much as the object of that withholding. Contracting our love energy cripples us. It's easy to see how contracted prejudiced people are. Being habitually judgmental makes us chronically tense.

It's said that the sun shines on the just and the unjust alike. Deservingness isn't an issue to unconditional love. We love not because of who others are but because of who we are. As far as the universe is concerned, everyone deserves love, even if they have little capacity to receive it. When society treats lawbreakers or military enemies with brutality, assuming that they deserve it, it debases itself and keeps a vicious cycle of hate going.

10 • CHOICE

A key concept in the Michael teachings is that all is choice. (See my book, *All Is Choice*, at my site.) We are constantly making choices, many times unconsciously. Taking ownership of our choices is essential to our happiness. When we believe we are primarily victims of things happening to us, we do not take full advantage of our ability to make choices and change our circumstances.

We often have a lot more choices than we realize. Fully considering our options is an important happiness tool. We are powerful when we make the choices that are ours to make, to the best of our ability, and let other people make the choices that are theirs to make. Other people's choices are usually out of our control and aren't our business, so it makes sense not to waste energy fussing about them, even when they are ill-advised or even karmic. It's fine to express our concerns when there's a chance they will be heard, and to prevent harm when possible, but others have the right to choose, even to choose to create karma. Being invested in the choices of others is certain to diminish our happiness. It tangles up our energy in theirs and dilutes it.

Other people's choices certainly affect us, but we usually can't do much about them. Sometimes we are in a position to control other people's behaviors, and this can be appropriate at times—for example, when raising children. But even with children, no one can control their internal choices. We can only control our own.

However, emanating unconditional love through

our emotions, truth through our intellect, and beauty through our body, to our highest ability, sets a tone that reminds others of the possibility of making more loving, truthful, and beautiful choices themselves. Love, truth, and beauty are the fundamental vibrations of the cosmos. Everything else comes from them. Negative energies are merely distorted, blocked, or immature expressions of them. Pure love, truth, and beauty, therefore, are more powerful than any other vibrations. The highest contribution we can make in any situation is to love, truthfully and beautifully.

Part II
HAPPINESS SKILLS

11 • FRAMING OUR EXPERIENCES

The way we frame our experiences is more important to our happiness than the experiences themselves. Theoretically, one could be happy (or at least peaceful) in any situation, although obviously some are more pleasant than others.

In a situation where one person is happy and another is unhappy, what is the difference? In Part I, we defined happiness as the free and refined expression of self. The first person's energy moves freely, to the extent possible, whereas the second person's doesn't. We saw that judgmentalness is one way we contract and block our energy flow; perhaps he judges his situation rather than embracing it as it is. There may be good reasons he doesn't like it—maybe it's not a good fit for him, or maybe it's just plain unpleasant. However, if it's not possible for him to leave or change it for the time being, he will be happier if he avoids contracting and gives whatever he can into it, framing it in the most positive possible way consistent with truth. The commitment to make the best of every situation and learn as much as possible from every lesson goes a long way toward creating happiness.

12 • TAKING ACTION

In these kinds of discussions, people often pose hypotheticals such as "What would you do in such-and-such a situation?" Translation: "You couldn't possibly be happy under those circumstances." One would not be happy *about* a negative circumstance, but those with strong happiness skills don't predominantly derive their happiness from external events. Paul Tillich defined joy as "the happiness of a soul which is lifted above every circumstance."

As to "What would you do?"—happiness comes from our inner state and *how* we do what we do, not necessarily what we do per se. Two people can take what appear to be the same actions, but with different intents, the energies and results are different. Furthermore, it isn't always possible to know ahead of time exactly what the most constructive thing to do would be in a future situation, but the better our problem-solving skills, the happier we are likely to be —they give us more confidence in our ability to handle whatever comes, and that brings greater equanimity. It's still possible to be happy even when we're in over our heads, especially if we acknowledge that and set about gaining skills and enlisting help. In any case, if we exercise whatever creative problem-solving capabilities we have and fully use our power of choice, we'll take the most effective actions available to us.

If we observe others doing harm and have the power to stop them, of course we would do that. If we can't, we would at least get out of the way if we're smart. If we take whatever action we choose with compassion, our life force continues to flow. If we have contempt, we stop its flow. If we view them as "other" – fundamentally different from us—we contract. If we see them as part of us, we expand. It is possible to effectively stop those doing harm and, at that same moment, have compassion for both the perpetrators and their victims.

Embracing "what is" is not the same as liking everything that happens. We naturally have preferences. We might say, for example, "I would really prefer not to be murdered. I took a lot of trouble setting up this lifetime and I don't want to have to do it over again!" That's perfectly reasonable. It is also perfectly reasonable to take actions to stop someone from murdering us or someone else. That is part of our right to choose, just as we have the right to form karma (although we avoid that if our intention is to get off the karmic wheel and be happy). Making laws to protect against violations is part of our collective right to choose. We stop the flow of our being only when we make a judgment that things aren't the way they should be when they *are* the way they are. It is an exercise in futility and a waste of time to resist how things are, because the present moment already exists and can't be changed—it's moving into the past. It's a better investment of our energies to focus instead on changing the next moment, not through resistance but by creating a more positive future through what we bring to this one.

13 • OUR GIFTS

One of the great happiness skills is recognizing the strengths behind behaviors, even if they are currently expressed in an immature way.

Let's say that someone is detail oriented—that's a gift. An immature or negative expression of that can be neurotic—obsessive/compulsive, for instance. It brings tension because it's too contracted. If he struggles with it and judges himself for being that way, he will become even more contracted, because judgmentalness contracts. Instead, if he accepts himself as he is, appreciating his detail-orientation as the gift that it is, he can relax with it and let it expand into equilibrium. He can find the place of "not too much and not too little," the balance point where the details he focuses on are those that will add something beneficial, letting go of the things that will not. This requires developing objective discernment: the ability to disconnect, step back, and observe rather than being blindly driven by the need for everything to be "perfect."

Some people are big-picture oriented. That's a gift, too—they can see the forest for the trees. Detail-oriented people generally focus on quality, and big-picture-oriented people, on quantity. We need both. Detail-oriented people polish works of art to a fine finish, making them more enjoyable. You probably want a detail-oriented person writing (or at least editing) what you read, so that it's not full of typos and unclarities that make reading more difficult. On the other hand, you probably want a big-picture-oriented person as a general contractor, someone

13 • OUR GIFTS

who can keep a project moving smoothly. Ideally, big-picture-oriented people are balanced enough to occasionally slow down and inspect details when necessary, even though their preference might be to quickly plow through tasks. It's all about balance—*balance* is a key happiness word—but the balance is in a different place for different people.

Some people are gifted with sensitivity. In order not to be frequently in pain, they may also need to develop strength. Those whose gift is strength may need to learn greater sensitivity so as not to use their strength in a ham-fisted manner.

Everyone has many gifts. A being doesn't become evolved enough to incarnate as a human without extraordinary amounts of development over eons. Unfortunately, we usually take them for granted and don't acknowledge them. Look for the gifts in those around you and express appreciation for them, especially to those who believe they don't have any. All our behaviors ultimately come from our gifts, whether in a mature, refined manner, or a crude, unpolished manner. By recognizing what our gifts are, we can evolve them.

14 • RESPECTING EMOTIONS

All emotions exist for a reason and have a place. Most spiritual and religious teachings have advocated denying or repressing unpleasant emotions because they didn't know what else to do with them (although this is beginning to change). Denied emotions are still there, so denial isn't helpful toward creating real happiness. Embracing our emotions as part of "what is" is the place to begin. Feel them fully. Observe them. What information do they give us? Are there any actions we need to take? Is there a part of us needing healing? When we've done all we can for now, we can let them go and move on. If they aren't done, they will come up again later to be embraced and understood from a higher vantage point.

When we experience violation, whether real or imagined, we naturally feel some combination of anger and fear. Anger moves toward it to try to stop it; fear moves away from it when stopping it doesn't seem possible. They are two sides of one coin, the masculine and feminine aspects of self-protection. Like yin/yang, fear is inside anger, and anger is inside fear. They can be useful in the presence of a threat, but problematic when stored long-term. Examining all our stored anger and fear, integrating their lessons, and releasing them will probably take a lifetime or more, but it is well worth doing, lightening our load and increasing our capacity for happiness.

15 • LIFE SKILLS

Ultimately, every life skill can contribute to our happiness. Communication skills, for example, can help us navigate the minefields of the world with more grace. If we can make our needs and feelings known to others in a positive way that doesn't put others on the defensive, we are more likely to resolve conflicts and create a better life.

Those who are growing consciously are constantly improving their life skills. Having enough skill and inner resources to handle what life brings us can help us relax and enjoy the ride. When life shows us that our skills and resources are lacking, that's the perfect time to work on developing them.

16 • UNDERSTANDING OUR DIFFERENCES

The Michael teachings help us understand why we're the way we are, the forces operating in our lives. That helps us release judgments of self and others. We are each a unique combination of strengths and weaknesses on the path of evolution. Without such understanding, we tend to assume that others are just like us, only wrong. Why don't they like the same things we do? Why do they behave in ways we never would? It turns out that there are a lot of good reasons, and the Michael teachings illuminate some pivotal ones.

17 • POSITIVE POLES

The happiness cornerstone of the Michael teachings is being in our positive poles more often and reducing our chief obstacle (aka chief feature—our biggest blind spot). As we do that, we gradually become happier people.

The positive poles are where those traits are in alignment with love, truth, and beauty. They're coming through in a free and refined way. In the negative pole, they are frozen by fear (and anger), either in contraction or expansion.

When we walk, our muscles expand *and* contract; if they didn't, we couldn't move—we'd be a blob. We need contraction as well as expansion, and we need to easily go back and forth between them. When a muscle is chronically contracted and can't move back into expansion, it hurts—it's stiff and sore. If it's chronically expanded, it's slack.

Most of our negative pole habits come from past experiences, either in this lifetime or previous ones, when we didn't have better tools—we didn't know more skillful, happier ways to deal with our challenges. Often due to trauma, we adopted limiting beliefs and froze into patterns of behavior that are less than optimal. In childhood, especially, our skills are naturally limited, but as we bring more consciousness to our negative poles, we can release old habits and evolve higher and higher versions of our overleaves.

In the negative pole of the goal of acceptance, for example, we fear not being accepted and become ingratiating, trying too hard to be liked and desperately afraid that if we're not, we'll die. Children naturally have a particularly high need to be accepted because if they're not, they could literally die—they can't fully take care of themselves. They don't yet have much capacity to feel secure in the absence of approval from others, so if love is frequently withheld, they may work overtime to try to get people to like them. Those with a goal of acceptance are particularly prone to this. Adults, however, have more capacity to develop a sense of security apart from other's acceptance of them, and can learn the positive pole of acceptance, which is ultimately about finding unconditional love and acceptance for others.

18 • BALANCING TRUE REST, PLAY, STUDY, AND WORK

We all have activities that are particularly restful for us—they rejuvenate us. Some activities are true play for us—they ground us and make us glad to be alive. Our true study is areas of learning that particularly nourish us intellectually. And our true work fits especially well with who we are and our life task. Having an adequate amount of each, in balance, is vital to our happiness. The balance is different for different people. Some need more rest, while others require more play (sages need more play than the other roles). Covering all these bases each week adds to our happiness. It is particularly common in our culture to neglect rest, play, or study when we get overly busy with our work, and that leads to reduced effectiveness.

19 • LIFE TASK

Each of us chose a life task before incarnating, and created a life plan to help us achieve it, as well as everything else on our "to do" list. We made agreements with other souls to help us accomplish them. When we intuitively sense and follow the direction of our soul, staying on our path, we're more likely to fulfill those agreements and complete our tasks. Life then goes more smoothly.

This doesn't mean we should blindly act on superficial feelings. That is a recipe for being tossed hither and yon. Staying on our path requires deep listening and wisdom, being a full, conscious collaborator with our soul. It does mean not letting our mind talk us out of what we know so that we go against the grain of self. If we examine our assumptions about what we should or have to do, we might find that they don't necessarily hold water.

20 • NINE NEEDS

The Michael teachings defines nine needs that we all have but prioritize differently based on what we most need in order to accomplish our life task. They are: security, adventure, freedom, expansion, power, expression, acceptance, communion, and exchange. Being aware of our priorities in this regard can help us be happier. For example, if you have a high adventure need, make sure that you have plenty of opportunity for adventure in your life, however you define that.

21 • EVOLUTION

Michael teaches that evolution is a slow, gradual, incremental process. At least it seems slow to us. From the Tao's point of view, it's neither slow nor fast—it's just what it needs to be. Even before our first lifetime on Earth, we had already evolved an enormous amount as a spark of the Tao. We are very large and complex, and there are a lot of layers involved in our evolution. It is not just our intellect that must learn, but all parts of us. If you are driving a large truck, turning it around will take longer than if you're driving a small car because there is more to turn.

Evolution is slower than it needs to be when we are blocked and blundering through life asleep. Being more conscious speeds up growth to a certain point, but at best, it still might not be as fast as we would like. Change can sometimes come quickly, but it can also take decades to make a dent in our major life issues. They would not be major life issues if they were easy; when their roots go deep, we have to address them one level at a time.

If you have been on the path of conscious growth for many years and could put who you were at age twenty next to who you are now, you would probably be astounded at how much you've grown. If you at age twenty had somehow been able to jump to where you are now, you would have been on cloud nine because of the huge rush. However, while it's happening, our growth is usually so gradual that we don't notice it. We tend, instead, to focus on all of the things that are still not yet what we want them to

21 • EVOLUTION

be.

Validation is an important word in the Michael teachings. If we can validate how far we've come, it helps us to be more patient with ourselves and the process. Notice when you've handled something better than you might have a year ago. No one gets to be a concert pianist or a conscious human overnight. If we consistently practice everyday, we'll get there. We can find happiness in incremental improvements.

22 • MODELING LOVE

Recognizing that something in ourselves is not the most we can be opens us to being more. When we compare it to our best models, we then have something we can strive to match. Doing this continually is the spiritual path.

The most important thing that any of us can do if we wish to help the planet is to be an example of what love, truth, and beauty look like, to the best of our ability. When people don't see positive role models around them, they don't know how to live a positive life. We all learn through role models. We need role models for happiness as well as for all the other qualities of essence. Most people don't know what they look like. What do we see on television? Where are role models for kindness, for example? Many so-called reality shows model meanness, selfishness, and manipulation—and glorify them. We need to see beautiful human beings. When we model qualities of essence, we have more impact than we know. Others don't usually tell us that they silently observe and take notes—that we made a difference—but those who are hungry for something higher do notice.

Part III

USING YOUR OVERLEAVES

23 • ROLES

The Michael teachings define seven *roles*, or soul types.

Servers thrive when they feel appreciated. We all thrive when we're appreciated but it's especially important for servers. It would be awkward to ask people to tell you that they appreciate you, but when someone does express appreciation, you can give positive reinforcement for that: "Wow, thank you! That makes me feel really good."

We tend to be self-deprecating about compliments. We all want to be loved, but then when love is expressed, we sometimes reject it. How much better to fully take it in. When we ask for things, we need to make space to receive them. By receiving appreciation and thanking the other person, we form a circuit. We make them feel good to know that they've made us feel good. As a result, they're probably going to express more appreciation for us in the future. That works a lot better than being a woebegone server who's always complaining "I slaved all day over a hot stove but nobody appreciates it!" That makes people want to leave.

Priests get depressed when they aren't inspired. All of us like to feel inspired, but for the other roles, it's not central. Different things inspire different people: being in nature, music, and meditating are examples. Meditation is great tool for happiness. It quiets us and allows spirit to take over for a while and relax, heal, and ground us. Priests who don't take time to recharge their inspiration languish. So stay inspired, priests!

Artisans thrive when they have a hobby, usually a craft. Artisan is the second most common role, accounting for twenty-two percent of the population. Obviously, twenty-two percent of people are not highly artistically gifted, but almost all artisans can get a lot of happiness out of doing something with their hands. It could be cooking or decorating—it doesn't have to be a handicraft.

Incidentally, almost anything you could say about an artisan is true of a sage to a lesser extent, and anything you can say about a sage is true of an artisan to a lesser extent. It works that way with the other axes, as well: warriors and kings, and servers and priests. The main difference between them is ordinality versus cardinality. (In the Michael teachings, the four *axes*, or basic qualities, are *inspiration, expression, action,* and *assimilation*.)

A big happiness tip for *sages* is laughter. I have a friend who is an old sage whose mother was mentally ill and severely abused her. When I first knew her, she never laughed. She smiled—she was as sweet as could be—but she didn't laugh. Her healing has been partly about regaining her ability to laugh. A sage who cannot laugh is in deep trouble.

You've probably heard the story of Norman Cousins who laughed himself to wellness by watching Marx Brothers movies and episodes of *Candid Camera*. He wrote, "I made the joyous discovery that ten minutes of genuine belly laughter had an anesthetic effect and would give me at least two hours of pain-free sleep," I channeled him as a priest with a discarnate sage essence twin, so sage was a secondary energy for him, but that sort of therapy would be especially good for sages.

Sages can also get a lot of happiness out of performing: playing in a band, acting in community theater, etc.

Warriors are the people who climb a mountain because it's there. (I look at pictures of a mountain while sitting on my Barcalounger because it's there. I don't need much challenge.) Warriors are not going to be happy if they don't have challenge and excitement: roller coasters, horror movies, athletics (both as participant and fan), etc. They also need worthwhile work.

Kings like to have big projects to sink their teeth into, preferably leading others, or a difficult skill they can master.

Scholars are pretty easy to keep happy as long as they have something to assimilate: books, movies, the Internet, etc. For moving centered scholars, travel can bring much happiness.

24 • GOALS

Goals are one of the *overleaves*, or personality traits we take on before each lifetime. Our goal is what motivates us, the kinds of experiences we seek.

Those in *reevaluation* enjoy quietude and nature. They consistently say things like "All I've ever wanted was a cottage by the shore or a cabin in the woods." Just not having too many demands on them is a happiness boost for them.

People in *growth* seek new things. They tend to be busy: they like to take new classes, read a new book, learn a new language, or eat a new cuisine. If they become overwhelmed, which they often do, they can benefit from sliding (temporarily moving to) to reevaluation. Sliding between growth and reevaluation is one of the most common sliding patterns among all of the overleaves—those in growth need to assimilate those new experiences, and those in reevaluation occasionally crave some stimulation, although not much.

Having high quality in our lives is especially important to those in *discrimination*, although it adds happiness for all of us. For example, if you want to watch TV, don't just watch what happens to be on. Give yourself a few minutes to research your options. Consider the DVDs you have, too, and pick something you'll really enjoy. When we keep watching something that's not very good due to inertia—we just don't feel like getting up and changing the channel—that degrades our happiness. It doesn't have to be *Masterpiece Classic*, just something that we really enjoy. Discrimination, like cynic, can be a difficult overleaf. In its negative pole, it can be excessively rejecting, such as driving other people away. But it need not manifest that way.

Those in *acceptance* especially appreciate agreeable circumstances and people; they avoid conflict, whereas some people are attracted to the excitement of it.

For those in *submission*, having something worthy of devotion, and having their devotion be respected, brings happiness.

Dominance is on the action axis, so it's about doing. Having an endeavor worth leading brings happiness for those in dominance.

Those in *flow* are happiest when they have a sense of freedom. They need to avoid getting stuck. Sliding to any of the other goals can help them overcome inertia and get moving again.

25 • ATTITUDES

Our attitude is what stands out to us when we look at the world.

The attitudes are the most flexible in the overleaves in that it's easier to borrow from others if we need to, although our native attitude forms our personality. For example, we can all benefit from sometimes being skeptical when that's called for, or from adopting the spiritualist's vision of possibility, the idealist's optimism, the pragmatist's practicality, the stoic's equanimity, and the realist's respect for facts. Such flexibility can help us avoid extremes. Most commonly, we slide to our opposite overleaf for balance, but with attitudes, the others are fairly easily accessed as well.

Those with the attitudes of cynic and skeptic can be just as happy as anyone else—there is no overleaf that is intrinsically unhappy when it is in the positive pole—but the pitfalls of their negative poles are particularly problematic, especially cynic, whose negative pole is denigration. In fact, cynic may be the most difficult overleaf. Still, some cynics happily do their positive pole of contradiction. A lot of comedians are skeptics and cynics. They have less need for optimism than the other attitudes, and generally don't miss it.

Any overleaf that is on the same side of the same axis as our role is more intense. For example, a sage idealist has a more pronounced experience of idealist than, say, a server, because sage and idealist are on the same side of the same axis. That's called a "natural overleaf." And if you're not an idealist but you're a sage, you still have a little bit of the idealist attitude built into who you are.

Cynic is a natural overleaf for warriors. I know a warrior cynic who can easily talk himself into a hopeless, black place, believing that everything is crap. That's an extreme expression of the negative pole.

We don't do harsher overleaves in many lifetimes but we do need to do them occasionally in order to have a balanced view of things. We need cynics—they test things for soundness. They challenge other people to prove that they're not pie in the sky. When spiritualists and idealists are full of inspiration and ideas about what could be, cynics come along and make sure that they hold water. They apply acid to metal to remove its tarnish, but in the negative pole there is so much acid that it eats through the metal and the thing is ruined. Few of us are in our positive poles all or even most of the time, so cynics will sometimes do denigration.

If we're on automatic pilot, we're likely to do our negative poles quite a bit. The more conscious we are, the better able we are to stay in our positive poles. As we do the work of bringing the light to bear on our shadows, the happier we can be. We are able to observe and understand our negative poles. We see that they are crude tools that don't work very well, that they are based in fear and make us unhappy. We increasingly choose to stay in our positive poles.

Stoics need peace to be happy.

Spiritualists need to share their vision of what could be, but they also need to make sure that it's grounded in reality—realists can help with that.

25 • ATTITUDES

Spiritualists are especially susceptible to taking on an inspiring vision that doesn't hold up, which can get them into trouble.

Skeptics need interesting things to explore. They can get bogged down in suspicion, their negative pole. The trick is to stay curious and open without bias either for or against.

Idealists are full of optimistic ideas for a better world. Similar to spiritualists, they need to ground their vision into the practical—pragmatists can help with that. Successfully instituting some of their ideas makes them happy.

Cynics appreciate when others are open to considering the issues they raise.

Realists like to know what the facts are in a situation but they can become earthbound. They can benefit from the inspirational input of spiritualists, just as spiritualists can be grounded by realists.

Pragmatists are happy when they find practical solutions, such as ways to reduce waste or to organize things better. They can become plodding and rigid, and benefit from the soaring ideas of idealists.

26 • MODES

Modes are about how we run our energy. The cardinal modes are expanded—they increase quantity; the ordinal modes are contracted—they increase quality. Occasionally sliding to the opposite overleaf, from ordinal to cardinal or vice versa, can help us find balance, and therefore happiness.

Passion mode is cardinal on the inspiration axis—it opens the floodgates to a greater quantity of inspirational energy. Its archetype is the big puppy. An example of it being out of balance (in the negative pole) is a person who throws herself into every love affair with so much abandon that she loses herself, until it inevitably breaks up. Happiness requires passion with healthy boundaries, which are the specialty of its opposite, reserve.

Being ordinal, *reserve* mode is the inner refinement of inspirational energy. Its archetype is the ballet dancer. When it is frozen in contraction, it is uptight. Happiness requires control with freedom, found in its opposite, passion.

Power mode is cardinal on the expression axis – it increases the weight of one's expressiveness. People in power mode may feel that they're just being themselves when others see them as being overbearing. Power is a natural overleaf for sages. A sage in power mode might seem like a larger-than-life diva, too loud and big in the negative pole. Happiness requires being aware of one's impact on others, careful about what one expresses, which is the specialty of its opposite, caution.

Caution mode can be too careful when in its negative pole, phobia. Happiness requires being in one's power, found in the positive pole of its opposite, authority.

Aggression mode is cardinal on the action axis—people in aggression do a lot. Since they naturally have dynamic energy, it's important for their happiness that they know when to rest. The negative pole is belligerence; particularly if they get too stressed or tired, they fly off the handle, losing their temper. Aggression is a natural overleaf for the king role, and it can look like king tyranny.

Aggression mode is balanced by *perseverance*, where one contracts on one task until it's completed. If it becomes stuck, unable to let go when it's time, it can find balance by borrowing from the dynamism of aggression mode to get one's energy moving again.

The neutral mode is *observation*, with a negative pole of surveillance. It can be balanced by sliding to any of the other modes, but especially helpful is minding one's own business. When we focus on making the choices that are ours to make, and leave others to make the choices that are theirs to make, it frees up a great deal of energy. The urge to gossip comes from instinctive center hardwiring designed to keep other members of our clan in line by judging them. Much of our growth comes from photographing when we're acting blindly from hardwiring and replacing that with more conscious and skillful approaches.

27 • CENTERS

We each have seven centers: emotional/higher emotional, intellectual/higher intellectual, physical/moving, and instinctive. One of the first concepts in the original Michael channelings was the need to balance our centers in order to be happy. That implies that we have cultivated all our centers enough so that when we react to a situation, we can use the correct tool for that situation. For instance, if somebody needs a hug, we react emotionally and hug them rather than intellectually, explaining how they should try to fix their circumstances. Someone lacking emotional development has a harder time doing that.

Our primary center (either intellectual, emotional, physical, or moving) is like a switchboard that can direct our next reaction to the most appropriate part of center. Even though we use one part of center habitually, our switchboard can direct us to a different part of our primary center when that's called for. The more balanced our centers are, the easier that will be.

We each have a weak link. I'm in the emotional part of intellectual center, so my weak link is my body. I have to be more deliberate about using it, such as exercising. I also have a passive body type, so getting my body in gear can be a challenge, but being disciplined about that balances me, so it's a boon to my happiness.

We use our higher centers both in everyday ways and for intense, peak experiences. We use our higher intellectual center to conceptualize, but also for

27 • CENTERS

transcendent aha's when we see eternal truths. We use our higher emotional center when we're feeling transpersonal emotions such as altruism, and also the highs that result when we feel one with the whole. We use our moving center to move, but when we're in the zone, such as during ecstatic dancing, we can feel bliss. Those peak higher-center experiences come from opening to our essence (our eternal nature), and to the essence of others. They are the epitome of happiness.

28 • OBSTACLES

Our chief obstacle is our greatest blind spot, what we most fear. It's an unconscious illusion we deeply believe on a gut level, that we will defend unto death until we become conscious of it. The seven are self-deprecation and arrogance, self-destruction and greed, martyrdom and impatience, and stubbornness. Overcoming our chief obstacle is the biggest thing we can do for our happiness. It is a huge subject, but I'll make a few comments here.

It's not useful to demonize the obstacles. It's not useful to demonize anything, because demonization originates from a false belief that something is not God or part of the whole—what is. If we see everything as a lesson or gift, we don't beat ourselves up about our obstacle. Getting in the habit of observing it with compassion and learning from it can contribute a great deal to our happiness. Michael refers to that as photographing it: recognizing it when it is operating in our lives, and knowing that it's an illusion even if we are not yet able to release it. We all have a bit of each of the obstacles in us, although one is dominant so we can better work on it.

Those in *self-deprecation* fear that they're inadequate. Knowing that that's an illusion, that we're all perfect as we are, and recognizing our strengths, can help. Putting oneself down is often seen as virtuous (especially compared to arrogance), but knowing one's strengths as well as one's weaknesses is not arrogance—it's just realism. If we don't believe in ourselves, we will sabotage all our efforts, which will only serve to seem to prove our inadequacy.

A good way to break the back of *arrogance* is to remember, when we feel critical of someone else, when we have done something similar and forgive ourselves for it.

Those in *self-destruction* fear a loss of self-control. They look for structure that they may have lacked as children, but as adults, we need to find our centering within. Becoming more conscious of our choices and developing inner balance is the long-term solution. Ultimately, stability only comes from grounding in the eternal.

Those in *greed* feel a hole inside them that nothing can fill. Gradually, by counting our blessings and validating what is already abundant in our life, we can break its hold.

Those in *martyrdom* fear that they aren't worthy and need to suffer in order to earn brownie points. Everyone is worthy and deserves the blessings of life. It is only our ability to know that and receive them that is at issue. Letting go of martyred role models is important here. Self-sacrifice is sometimes called for, but win-win is a higher paradigm.

With *impatience*, if we're running late once again, rather than frantically speeding up, we can do the opposite and come into the present moment in a relaxed way in the awareness that all is well, even if we'll be late. Calmly considering our choices and letting go of doing things that can wait help us work smarter.

Stubbornness is the most common obstacle, and because it's on the neutral (assimilation) axis, it tends to be especially invisible to those who hold it. "What me? I'm not stubborn! I'm just standing up for myself. Nobody is going to tell me what to do!" Noticing the feeling of digging in our heels helps a lot. Gradually opening up and discovering that it's safe to let others make some decisions that affect us, and that it's safe to change our point of view—that change can be for the better—softens stubbornness.

For more on the obstacles, read José Stevens' book *Transforming Your Dragons*.

29 • BODY TYPES

Body types are the influences of the celestial bodies on our physical bodies. There are seven main ones. Four (*saturnian, venusian, jovial,* and *solar*) are positive charged, meaning that their focus is external. They tend to be better at letting things slide of their back because they don't take things in as much. Three of the body types *(lunar, mercurial* and *martial)* are negative charged. They take in things more and are more easily hurt. They need to learn how to manage their higher sensitivity. Negative types can have as much happiness as positive, but they have to be more careful about protecting themselves, which they instinctively do.

Here we are addressing our body's hardwiring. One could have a positive body type but have high mental/emotional sensitivity. Also, artisans and sages are the most sensitive of the roles because of their multiple inputs, or psychic receivers.

We generally have a combination of two or three body-type influences working together. A person's body could be half positive and half negative, in which case she's in the middle. But someone with, say, ninety percent negative influences is likely to be hypersensitive and feel everything, especially with a high amount of lunar influence, which is also passive and feminine, so it doesn't have built-in defenses. Therefore, lunars need to be alone a lot, and especially benefit from learning not to take in other people's energies. However, becoming skillful in handling energy requires all of us to discern and let go of what is not ours and maintain the sanctity of our aura. Humanity's tangled karmic energies make it hard to know who we are and create happiness.

Having a positive body type gives you an initial leg up with happiness, but where positive types get into trouble is by being oblivious. Saturnian/venusian combinations, for example, tend to be easygoing. If they let trouble signs slide off their back, failing to engage with them, they can slam into a wall.

Body types are also differentiated by being either active or passive, and either masculine or feminine. Active types are more often drawn to exercise, which adds to happiness by generating endorphins. However, they are less comfortable than passive types when required to sit still. Whatever our configuration, we need to learn how to manage it in a way that's in balance.

CONCLUSION

The Michael teachings are one tool that can help us be more self-aware. By comparing our present experience to the yardstick of happiness—a free and refined expression of self—we can gradually become happier.

BACK MATTER

ABOUT THE AUTHOR

SHEPHERD HOODWIN has been channeling since 1986. He also does intuitive readings, mediumship, past-life regression, healing, counseling, and channeling coaching (teaching others to channel). He has conducted workshops on the Michael teachings throughout the United States and Europe.

Shepherd is a graduate of the University of Oregon. He lives in Laguna Niguel, California.

https://shepherdhoodwin.com

TWITTER:
@shepherdh
@EnlightenNitwit

FACEBOOK:
https://www.facebook.com/shepherd.hoodwin
https://www.facebook.com/shepherd.hoodwin.author/
https://www.facebook.com/JourneyOfYourSoul/
https://www.facebook.com/EnlightenmentforNitwits/

shepherdhoodwin@gmail.com

Summerjoy Press
99 Pearl
Laguna Niguel CA 92677-4818

OTHER BOOKS BY SHEPHERD HOODWIN

Available at https://shepherdhoodwin.com/book/

All Is Choice

Few realize how profound, multi-faceted, and far-reaching the concept of choice is in our spiritual growth. This short book explores topics such as what is and is not our right to choose, our power as creators and the limits of our reality creation, how consciousness expands, and much more.

Being in the World

This insightful book explores practical spirituality. Topics include aging, karma, time, and religion.

Compassion for Evil
A Metaphysical View

Compassion for Evil explores the nature of evil from the soul's point of view, and how we can skillfully deal with it as lightworkers.

Embracing What Is
Spiritual Keys to Happiness

This book is an abridged version of *Happiness and the Michael Teachings*, without technical Michael teachings terminology. A free version is available at Smashwords.com.

Energy Literacy
How to Perceive and Take Charge of Your Spiritual Well-Being

Energy Literacy is an introduction to how to perceive our energy field and release negativity. Topics include chakras, contracts, vows, cording, entities, implants, psychic attack, earthbound souls, soul retrieval, and more.

Enlightenment for Nitwits
The Complete Guide

This hilarious metaphysical/self-help humor collection will appeal to Oprah and Dave Barry fans as well as those with more esoteric interests. In a style reminiscent of comedian Steven Wright, it's full of wry one-liners along with longer, hilariously mind-bending pieces on a wide range of subjects, tied together by the idea of clueless humans trying to find enlightenment.

"I love *Enlightenment for Nitwits*! It is the funniest book I have read in several decades. If laughter leads to enlightenment, it will certainly do it. Nothing—thank God—is sacred in this delightful spoof on life in general."
—C. Norman Shealy, M.D., author of *Life Beyond 100*

OTHER BOOKS BY SHEPHERD HOODWIN

Growing Through Joy

This thought-provoking book explores the nature of personal growth.

Healing the Gut
A Crib Sheet for Eliminating SIBO

This short book offers tips for those with digestive problems and related diseases, focusing on the Specific Carbohydrate Diet.

Journey of Your Soul
A Channel Explores the Michael Teachings

This is the most in-depth discussion of the Michael teachings to date. It may also be the first analytical study of channeling written by a channel. It has forewords by John Friedlander, co-author of *Psychic Psychology*, and Jon Klimo, author of *Channeling: Investigations on Receiving Information from Paranormal Sources*. Klimo writes, "*Journey of Your Soul* may well be the best (Michael) book of them all due to its clarity, thoroughness, and detail, and thanks to the fact that the author, an exceptionally clear-headed Michael channel himself, brings real integrity and authenticity to our understanding of Michael in particular and to the channeling process in general."

Loving from Your Soul
Creating Powerful Relationships

This inspiring, transformative book explores the nature of love itself as well as practical matters of relationships. One reader wrote, "There are phrases that are so inspiring that I wrote them down to refer to when I need them. I am looking forward to reading this book again and again."

Meditations for Self-Discovery
Guided Journeys for Communicating with Your Inner Self

This is a beautiful collection of forty-five vivid, often pastoral, guided imagery meditations channeled from Shepherd's essence. There are many meditation recordings available, but this is one of the first collections of meditations in book form that can be read to oneself or others. Teachers and group leaders would find it particularly useful.

Opening to Healing

This uplifting book explores the spiritual aspect of healing.

Unconditional Love in Politics
Or Have You Hugged a Republican/Democrat Today?

Is unconditional love in politics an oxymoron? Thus far, it's been a rare commodity if it's ever been there. This book explores what you can do about it, as well as why both right and left have useful parts to play in our evolution, the factors that influence a person's tilt to the right or left, and what unconditional love might look like in this sphere.

Why We're Attracted
Spiritual, Psychological and Physical Elements That Draw Us to Others

Just why are we attracted to some people and not to others? This book explores a multitude of factors on three levels: spiritual, psychological, and physical. Topics include agreements, life path, soul chemistry, male/female energy ratio, celibacy, body-type attraction, sexual orientation, monogamy, and polyfidelity.

REVIEWS

I'm someone to whom happiness doesn't come all that easily. The Michael teachings and Shepherd's work are a great help, though. This book is full of spiritual wisdom and beautiful insights into the true nature of happiness and joy, and what keeps us from experiencing that. Especially for those who are familiar with the Michael teachings, it offers a lot of practical information. Among others, for each goal, overleaf and body type, Shepherd gives background information and describes what can enhance happiness.

I found this book to be eye-opening, practical, and loving. It gives clear answers to situations I'm dealing with, and it's worth reading several times. I'm happy I bought it!

Printed in Great Britain
by Amazon